RIVERS THROUGH TIME

Settlements of the River
NILE

Rob Bowden

www.heinemann.co.uk/library

Visit our website to find out more information about **Heinemann Library** books.

To order:
☎ Phone 44 (0) 1865 888066
▤ Send a fax to 44 (0) 1865 314091
▣ Visit the Heinemann Bookshop at www.heinemann.co.uk/library to browse our catalogue and order online.

First published in Great Britain by Heinemann Library, Halley Court, Jordan Hill, Oxford OX2 8EJ, part of Harcourt Education. Heinemann is a registered trademark of Harcourt Education Ltd.

Editorial: Jilly Attwood and Kate Bellamy
Design: Richard Parker and
    Tinstar Design Ltd (www.tinstar.co.uk)
Illustrator: Stephen Sweet (SGA) and Jeff Edwards
Picture Research: Ruth Blair and Ginny Stroud-Lewis
Production: Séverine Ribierre
Originated by Dot Gradations Ltd
Printed in China by WKT Company Limited

ISBN 0 431 12044 7 (hardback)
08 07 06 05 04
10 9 8 7 6 5 4 3 2 1

ISBN 0 431 12049 8 (paperback)
10 09 08 07 06
10 9 8 7 6 5 4 3 2 1

British Library Cataloguing in Publication Data
Bowden, Rob
Settlements of the River Nile - (Rivers through time)
962
A full catalogue record for this book is available from the British Library.

Acknowledgements
The publishers would like to thank the following for permission to reproduce photographs:
Alamy pp. 18, 43; Ancient Art and Architecture Collection pp. 19, 31; Axiom p. 21; Corbis pp. 4, 5, 11, 15, 17, 33, 37; Corbis pp. 34, 36 (Paul Almasy), 25 (Yann Arthus Bertrand), 14 (Lloyd Cluff), 27 (Digital Image/NASA), 20, 30 (Robert Holmes), 9 (Michael Nicholson), 12 (Carmen Redondo), 29 (Reza Webistan); Images of Africa pp. 40, 41; Pictures p. 42; Robert Harding p. 23; Still Pictures p. 13; Sylvia Cordaiy p. 39; The Art Archive pp. 24, 35.

Cover photograph reproduced with permission of Picture Colour Library.

Contents

Words in bold, **like this,** are explained in the Glossary.

Introducing the River Nile

The majestic Nile

The River Nile is the longest river in the world. It stretches for an incredible 4132 miles (6650 kilometres) and passes through seven countries. The Nile is actually two rivers – the White Nile and the Blue Nile. They join to become a single river, the Nile, at Khartoum in Sudan. In this book we focus on the White Nile, as this is the longer of the two rivers. It also has more **settlements** along its length than the Blue Nile.

As well as being the king of rivers, the Nile is also sometimes known as the river of kings. This refers to the **pharaohs** of ancient Egypt who ruled the Nile Valley for thousands of years and built great kingdoms. The remains of these kingdoms can be seen in modern-day Egypt. They include the pyramids of Giza, near Cairo, and the temples and Valley of the Kings in Luxor. The ancient Egyptians thrived alongside the Nile because of its life-giving waters. Every year the river would flood and deposit a layer of thick **fertile** soil across the Nile valley.

An ancient Egyptian wall painting of a husband and wife ploughing fields by the River Nile (shown at the bottom of the picture).

The White Nile crashes over Kabalega Falls, also known as Murchison Falls, in Northern Uganda.

River glossary

Confluence – the point where two rivers join.

Delta – where the river joins the sea.

Mouth – the ending point of a river.

Reaches – used to describe sections of the river (upper, middle and lower reaches).

River course – the path followed by a river from source to mouth.

Source – the starting point of a river.

Tributary – a river or stream that joins another (normally bigger) river.

The rich soils brought great harvests to the farmers of the Nile valley. The Nile also provided a trade route between the Mediterranean Sea and the heart of Africa. Goods such as ivory, gold and spices were traded up and down the river.

The Nile is as important to the people living alongside it today as it was in ancient times. It continues to provide water for farming and remains an important transport route. It brings them new benefits too. These include electricity generated by the force of its waters, and tourists who come to marvel at the river, its people and their history.

From source to mouth

Although people have lived along the Nile for thousands of years, its **source** remained a subject of great mystery, which was solved in 1858 by John Hannington Speke, a British explorer. He identified the start of the White Nile as Ripon Falls in present-day Uganda. Here the Nile flows out of an enormous lake, which Speke named Lake Victoria after the British queen of the time. However, further explorations have shown that the ultimate source of the Nile is the Kagera River in Burundi. It is from here that the Nile is measured as the world's longest river.

In its upper **reaches** the White Nile switches between a crashing, fast-moving river, and a much slower, more gentle river. The fast-flowing sections are caused by a series of rapids, where hard rocks lie across the riverbed and send the water crashing over them. The slower sections form much wider channels of water. In northern Uganda the White Nile drops over the Kabalega Falls. It then carves its way through the mountains of southern Sudan before almost slowing to a halt in the Sudd. This is a giant swamp, full of vegetation that clogs the river and sends its waters spilling over the level land around it.

In its middle reaches the White Nile leaves the Sudd and flows slowly for around 500 miles (800 kilometres). In Sudan's capital, Khartoum, it is joined by the Blue Nile, which begins at Lake Tana in the highlands of Ethiopia. After cascading over Tis Abay Falls (the highest on the Nile, at 45 metres), the Blue Nile cuts through the highlands in deep gorges. The fast-moving waters carry thousands of tons of **sediment** with them as they **erode** the land around them. Although shorter than the White Nile, the Blue Nile contributes around 70 per cent of the river that eventually flows into Egypt.

Downstream of Khartoum the river is simply known as the Nile. It is joined by another major tributary, the Atbara River, before it reaches Egypt. Today, the Nile enters Egypt through Lake Nasser. This lake was formed by the Aswan High Dam, which holds back the Nile and controls the release of its waters into Egypt. Below the dam the Nile passes through a narrow valley, with desert on either side of it. Shortly after passing through Cairo the Nile splits into two channels known as the Damietta and Rosetta. Once there were seven channels, but over time water has been diverted into just two so that more land can be used for farming and for settlements. These form the **delta** region of the Nile, where it eventually meets the Mediterranean Sea.

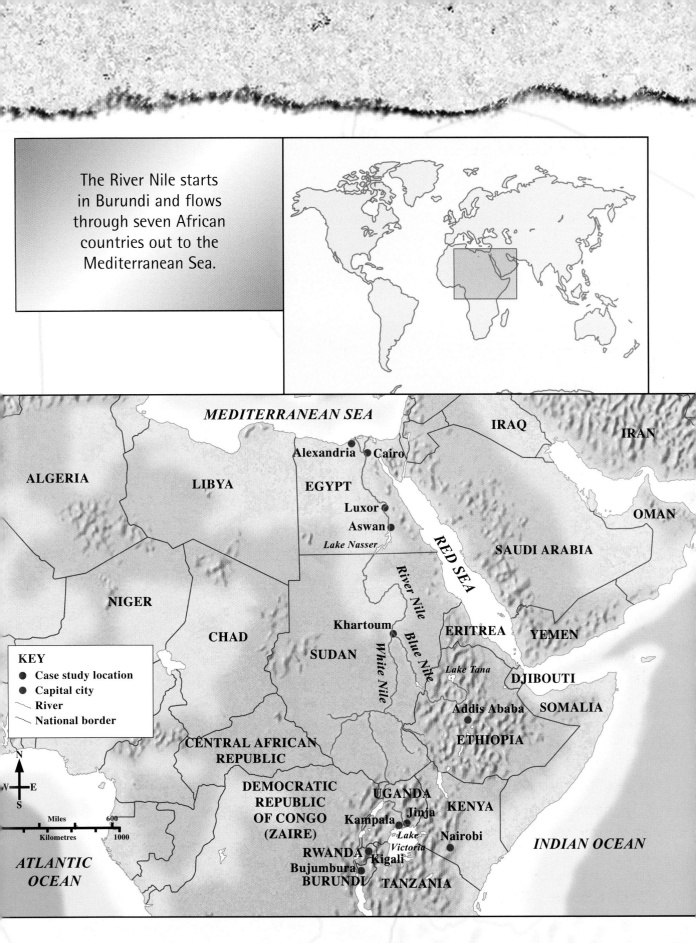

The River Nile starts in Burundi and flows through seven African countries out to the Mediterranean Sea.

MEDITERRANEAN SEA

IRAQ

IRAN

ALGERIA

LIBYA

EGYPT

Alexandria   Cairo

Luxor

Aswan

Lake Nasser

RED SEA

SAUDI ARABIA

OMAN

NIGER

CHAD

SUDAN

Khartoum

River Nile

Blue Nile

White Nile

ERITREA

YEMEN

Lake Tana

DJIBOUTI

KEY
● Case study location
● Capital city
～ River
～ National border

Addis Ababa

SOMALIA

ETHIOPIA

CENTRAL AFRICAN
REPUBLIC

N
W   E
S

Miles   600
Kilometres   1000

DEMOCRATIC
REPUBLIC
OF CONGO
(ZAIRE)

UGANDA

Kampala   Jinja

KENYA

Nairobi

Lake
Victoria

INDIAN OCEAN

ATLANTIC
OCEAN

RWANDA   Kigali

Bujumbura
BURUNDI   TANZANIA

Settlements along the Nile

Apart from the mountainous stretches of its upper reaches, the Nile has settlements along most of its length. The majority of these settlements are small farming and fishing villages located close to the banks of the Nile. A few of them have developed into larger towns, where people gather to trade goods. In Uganda, for example, Jinja has become a major market for farm produce and for fish caught in Lake Victoria.

Most of the major settlements along the Nile are in its middle and lower reaches. Much of this region was historically flooded each year by the annual flow of the river. As the flood waters subsided they left behind a fresh layer of **nutrient**-rich sediment, brought down from the Ethiopian highlands. This provided the best farmland in the whole of Africa and naturally attracted people to settle there. The Nile was also a source of water for farming and home use, and provided a transport route for the movement of goods and people. Today, the annual flooding of the Nile is controlled by a series of dams, but the river remains a major centre of population, from Khartoum to its **mouth**.

What's in a name?

*The River Nile is known by many different names from source to mouth. In its first section, for example, it is known as the 'Victoria Nile', whilst in southern Sudan it is known as 'Bahr al-Jabal', meaning 'mountain Nile'. The ancient Egyptians knew the river as 'Ar' or 'Aur', which means black. It was so-called because of the black sediment that was carried by the river when it was in flood. The modern name 'Nile' is thought to have developed from a **Semitic** word 'nahal', which means river valley. In Greek this became 'Neilos' ('Nilus' in Latin) and over time this changed to give the name Nile.*

Surrounded by desert to either side, the Nile provides a narrow strip of life through an otherwise barren landscape. Great cities such as Cairo, Alexandria and Khartoum dominate this area, but there are hundreds of smaller settlements in between, such as Aswan and Luxor.

In this book we will explore the major settlements along the River Nile. We will follow a journey through time, starting with Aswan and ending in Jinja – a town where plans are being made that may change the Nile forever. We will look at why these settlements were founded and how they have changed. We will consider what those settlements are like today and how they might change in the future. Most importantly, we will discover how the settlements are linked to the Nile and the lives of the people living there.

The calm waters of the Nile pass through the centre of Cairo – the largest city in Africa.

Aswan: the great dam

City of elephants

It is difficult to say exactly when the first **settlement** appeared at
Aswan. One thing is certain though – it has been settled for a very
long time. Some of the earliest records for Aswan suggest that it
dates back to at least 3000 BC. Whatever the precise date, Aswan
has always been an important centre for trade. Its name comes from
the ancient Egyptian word 'Swen', which means market. Aswan was
in a perfect location for trade as it was the furthest point south that
boats could reach by sailing up the Nile. A set of rapids known as
the First Cataract blocked their passage further upriver. The ancient
Egyptians believed that these falls were in fact the **source** of the Nile.

The earliest settlement at Aswan was on an island in the middle
of the Nile called Elephantine Island. This unusual name comes
from its ancient Egyptian name, Abu, meaning elephant. Some
believe this refers to the granite boulders in the water around the
island that look a bit like bathing elephants. Other experts believe
that the island was once an important centre for trading ivory.

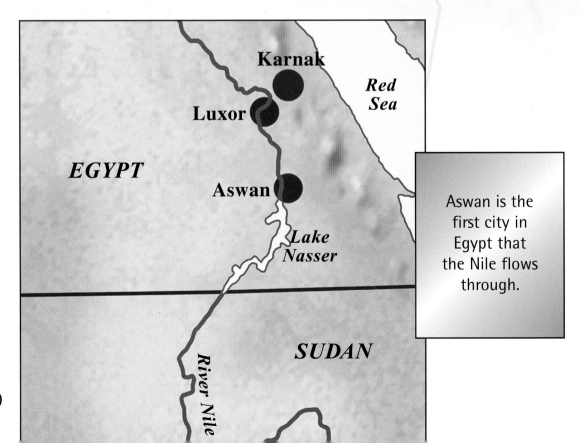

Aswan is the first city in Egypt that the Nile flows through.

Traders also brought gold, leather, precious stones, ebony and spices. Elephantine Island became an important southern capital for the Egyptians. As well as being the gateway to the riches of Africa it also provided a base to protect Egypt from southern invasions. Most importantly, however, the island was ideally located to monitor the annual flooding of the Nile. This was done using a device known as a Nilometer.

A Nilometer is a steep staircase cut into the side of the island and down into the Nile. The 90 regularly shaped steps acted as markers to measure the rise and fall of the river. The level of the flood recorded at the Nilometer was used to predict the future harvest in the Nile valley downstream. This helped the Egyptians calculate the amount of tax that farmers had to pay to the **pharaohs**.

Today, Elephantine Island and its Nilometer are a major tourist attraction. **Archaeologists** are also working on the island to learn more about the ancient origins of Aswan. They are slowly unearthing the remains of an old town at the southern end of the island. This has revealed a temple to Satis, a goddess linked to the Nile. Her husband, Khnum, the lord of the Nile flood, was believed to guard the waters of the Nile at this point of the river.

11

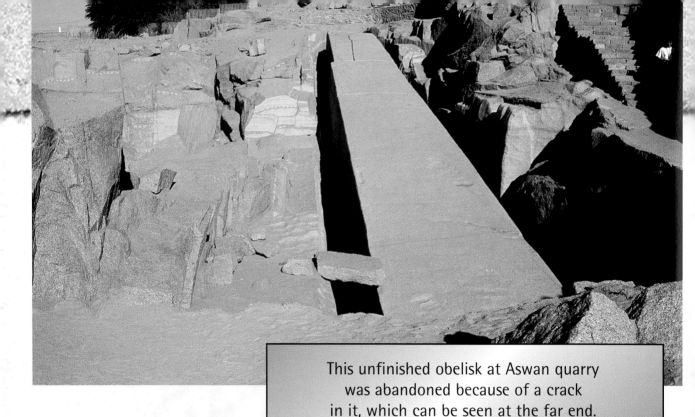

This unfinished obelisk at Aswan quarry
was abandoned because of a crack
in it, which can be seen at the far end.

Land of granite

Aswan played a key role in the construction of many of Egypt's
greatest temples. It was the main source of granite, a hard rock
used to build many of their finest buildings. The granite around
Aswan was particularly valued because of its many different
shades: grey, black, red and even pink. The pyramids at Giza
(see page 31), built between 2613 and 2494 BC, were some of
the first to include granite quarried around Aswan. Once cut
from the quarry the granite would have been taken downstream
by boat along the Nile. Without the river it would have been
almost impossible to transport such heavy pieces of rock.

The most impressive pieces to be transported by river were
two giant **obelisks**. An obelisk is a square-sided pillar that
narrows to a point at the top. The obelisks were erected by
Queen Hatshepsut, who ruled Egypt between 1490 and 1468 BC.
She ordered that they should be carved from a single piece
of Aswan's best pink granite. A team of workers took seven
months to complete the obelisks, which each stood nearly
30 metres tall and weighed 323 tonnes. The obelisks were
transported to Luxor by river before being erected in the
temple of Karnak in 1475 BC. They were the tallest obelisks in
Egypt and one of them still stands in the temple ruins today.

Nile feluccas are part of the Nile scenery around Aswan. Once used for trade, they are now more commonly used to take tourists out on the river.

Another obelisk remains on its side in an Aswan quarry, still attached to the bedrock beneath it. This unfinished obelisk would have been the biggest ever made. If completed it would have stood around 42 metres high and weighed as much as 1190 tonnes. The obelisk appears to have been abandoned because a crack developed in the rock as it was being carved. Although unfinished, the obelisk has given archaeologists a chance to see the skills used to create such magnificent objects.

Nile feluccas

The river in Aswan is crowded with graceful sailboats called feluccas. Today, many of them carry tourists on trips around the islands or from one bank of the Nile to the other. In the past, though, feluccas would have been the main form of transport up and down the Nile. They would have transported goods to and from the market in Aswan as far back as the time of the pharaohs. Their simple design is so suited to life on the Nile that it has changed little in thousands of years. For many visitors to Egypt a felucca is still the best way to visit the many temples that line the Nile between Aswan and Cairo.

Damming the Nile

Aswan is still an important market town in Egypt today. Its market, or souq, attracts traders who have travelled along the Nile or across the surrounding desert. However, the town is best known for its dams across the Nile. The first dam was completed in 1902 by the British, who were in control of much of Egypt between 1882 and 1952. Important at the time, the old dam is now overshadowed by the Aswan High Dam. This massive dam took eleven years to build and was finished in 1971. It is 2.2 miles (3.6 kilometres) long and its main wall is 111 metres tall and 980 metres wide at its base. Behind the dam, an artificial lake, Lake Nasser, was created that stretches upstream for 310 miles (500 kilometres) into neighbouring Sudan.

The Aswan High Dam was considered a great triumph for Egypt. Flooding was controlled, and water was taken from the dam for new areas of farmland. The dam also allowed

The Aswan High Dam controls the Nile waters and provides much-needed electricity for Egypt.

3000BC	2613-2494BC	1475BC
Probable founding of Aswan.	Pyramids at Giza are built using granite from Aswan.	Queen Hatshepsut's obelisks transported to Luxor for the Temple of Karnak.

Farming and trading of goods like spices takes place alongside more modern industries in Aswan.

electricity to be generated by the water passing through the dam. The electricity and the guaranteed water supplies attracted industries to Aswan. Today, these include cement production, a sugar refinery, copper and steel factories and a chemical fertilizer plant. New workers settled in Aswan and the town's population rapidly grew. Before the dam was finished Aswan had a population of around 40,000 people, but now it is almost 250,000.

The Aswan High Dam is vital for Egypt's economy and people, especially the millions living downstream of it. Today, around 70 million people are dependent on Aswan and its control of the Nile.

Not all good news

*The Aswan High Dam has not been all good news. The Nubians who once lived in the valley south of Aswan were forced to move as Lake Nasser was formed. Their houses and many ancient temples were lost beneath the waters. Downstream of the dam, **nutrients** that once fertilized farmers' fields during the annual floods no longer arrive. Farmers are now dependent on chemical fertilizers. The use of water for **irrigation** has also caused a rise in the **water table** under Egypt's farmland. This has brought salts to the soil surface and caused declines in crop growth in some areas. The effects of the Aswan High Dam are even felt as far away as the Mediterranean Sea. There, sardine catches have fallen dramatically, as nutrients are no longer carried into the sea by the annual Nile floods.*

AD1882-1952	1902	1971
British in control of Aswan.	First dam at Aswan completed by the British.	Aswan High Dam is completed.

Luxor: city of kings

A royal city

Luxor is at the heart of Egypt's tourist industry. It is visited by thousands of tourists every day. They come to see the remains of ancient palaces and temples that once graced this royal city. In ancient times the **settlement** was actually known as Thebes. This name is sometimes still used to describe the area around the modern town of Luxor. In the early period of Egyptian civilization, known as the Old Kingdom, Thebes was little more than a small farming village on the banks of the Nile. It was only later that it developed into an important city. These ancient Egyptian periods are known as the Middle Kingdom (2040–1730 BC) and the New Kingdom (1552–1069 BC).

The first rulers of the Middle Kingdom came from around Thebes and chose to make it the centre of their new kingdom. The land around Thebes was plentiful and **fertile**. Its location also allowed the new rulers to control both upper Egypt (upstream) and lower Egypt (downstream). The new rulers worshipped a local god called Amun-Re. Amun was the king of all Egyptian gods and was closely linked to the Sun god **Re**. The worship of Amun-Re soon spread across the state of Egypt, and Thebes became the spiritual centre of Egypt.

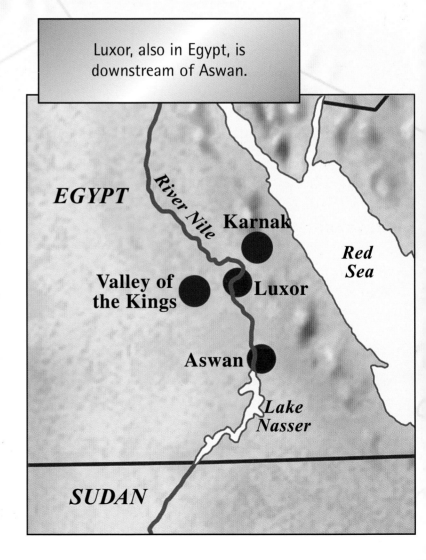

Luxor, also in Egypt, is downstream of Aswan.

The Nile runs through the middle of Luxor. The city is on one side, with mountains behind, and the other side is mostly farm land.

The importance of religion

The Nile divided Thebes into two halves – eastern and western Thebes. Eastern Thebes was the city of the living. It was here that the Sun rose each morning, bringing new life to the river and its people. The **pharaohs** built great temples to honour Amun-Re and the life-giving Sun. On the opposite side of the Nile was western Thebes. Here the Sun would set each evening behind the cliffs that line the edge of the Nile valley. The Egyptians chose western Thebes to be the burial place for their dead. They believed that by burying their dead here the Sun god would safely transport their dead into the underworld where they could enjoy eternal life. It is for this reason that western Thebes is often known as the 'city of the dead' or the '**necropolis** of Thebes'. Western Thebes became the home of the priests and of the craftspeople who built the great **mortuary** temples of the pharaohs. The west bank was also an important farming area, as it was in the flood plain of the Nile.

17

Temples of the Nile

In ancient times the Nile linked both halves of Thebes, with boats carrying people and goods between the two. Most boats would have been made of **papyrus**, as this was freely available along the banks of the Nile. The ancient Egyptians also built stronger barges for transporting heavy goods and for use in elaborate festivals. These were made of wood, much of which was imported from neighbouring countries such as Lebanon. These barges enabled the Egyptians to transport stone for building the temples of Thebes. Without the Nile the temples may never have been built.

To move the stone as close to the temples as possible, the pharaohs ordered canals to be built. These artificial channels connected the temples to the Nile and would have had busy **wharves** where building materials were unloaded from the river. The remains of some of the canals and wharves are still clearly visible today.

As well as being used to transport stone, the Nile itself provided an important building material – mud. Nile mud was made into bricks that were baked hard in the Sun. These Nile bricks were used to build temples as well as houses. The main temple in Luxor is the temple of Amun-Re. This enormous temple is better known as the temple of Karnak. It is located alongside the Nile, just to the north of the centre of Luxor. The temple itself underwent great changes over a period of around 1300 years, as different pharaohs came and went. Some of them tore bits down, whilst others rebuilt sections or added new ones. **Archaeologists** believe that most of the temple was built by the pharaohs of the New Kingdom, but parts of it date back almost 4000 years.

This is a wall painting showing the Opet festival during the Nile floods.

The Opet festival

The great city of Thebes owed its wealth to the life-bringing waters of the Nile. Each year the ancient Egyptians would celebrate this with the Opet festival at the peak of the Nile flood. The centre piece of the festival was an ornate sacred barge. The barge was used to carry a statue of the god Amun-Re from the main temple at Karnak to the Luxor Temple upstream. Here he was reunited with his wife, Mut (which means mother), and his son Khonsu, the god of the Moon and of healing. The festivities included dancing, acrobats, flowers and sacrifices to the gods. After a few days the sacred barge sailed downstream again and Amun-Re was returned to his temple in Karnak. In another annual festival Amun-Re was carried across the Nile to visit the temples of the dead pharaohs.

Tourist hotspot

Luxor – the modern name for Thebes – comes from the Arabic 'Al-Uqsur', which means the palaces or the castles. This refers to the many fine temples and palaces that were built by the ancient Egyptians. Today these attract thousands of tourists to visit Luxor every year. Besides the grand temple at Karnak, most visitors come to see the famous Valley of the Kings – where the pharaohs of the New Kingdom were buried. They took with them great treasures for their eternal life in the underworld. Unfortunately most of the tombs have been looted (robbed) and all that remains today are their beautifully painted walls.

The Valley of the Kings has two parts, the East Valley and the West Valley. The East Valley has most of the tombs of the New Kingdom pharaohs, and attracts more tourists.

2040–1069BC	2000BC	c1550BC
Era of the Middle Kingdom and New Kingdom. Thebes becomes an increasingly important city.	Earlier parts of the temple of Karnak are built.	The first Opet festival takes place.

Nile cruise boats and yachts moor alongside the Temple of Karnak in Luxor.

One tomb did survive the looters though – the tomb of Tutankhamun. This was discovered in 1922 by British archaeologist Howard Carter. Inside the tomb were great treasures, many of them made of solid gold. The treasures made the Valley of the Kings world famous and turned them into a major tourist attraction. The treasures themselves are now on show in the Egyptian Museum in Cairo.

Luxor is today dominated by tourism, with the Nile at its centre. Nile cruise boats are one of the most popular ways to see the Nile and the attractions that line its banks. Luxor is the most popular destination for the cruise boats, though most also call at Aswan. Each cruise boat brings hundreds of new tourists into Luxor. In the peak season the boats may be lined several deep along the busy waterfront. Feluccas (see page 13) offer a more basic and traditional way to cruise along the Nile, but few tourists travel in this way now.

However the tourists arrive (there is also a train station and international airport in Luxor) they bring welcome jobs to the people of Luxor. Many of

Luxor's people depend on the tourist industry for their income. This means that in many ways they still depend on the Nile, much as their ancestors would have done. Without the great gift of the Nile, the great temples of Luxor may never have been built and there would be little for the tourists to see in this royal city.

c1325BC	c747–645BC	AD1922
Tutankhamun dies in his late teens.	Thebes is capital of Egypt.	Howard Carter discovers the tomb of Tutankhamun.

Alexandria: learning and farming

Gateway to the Nile

Alexandria is located at the western end of the giant Nile **delta**. At one time the Nile delta would have been part of the Mediterranean Sea, into which the Nile flows. Over millions of years the **sediment** carried downstream by the Nile filled in the delta region and pushed the sea back. Across the delta region today this sediment is between 15 and 23 metres thick and is rich in **nutrients** brought down from the Ethiopian highlands. This makes the soils of the Nile delta the most fertile in Africa and some of the best farmland in the world. Since ancient times **settlements** were established here to take advantage of its rich soils. The Nile delta remains the most important farming area in Egypt today and is where most of the country's population live.

Alexandria, in Egypt, is at the mouth of the Nile.

FACT

Delta is the name for the Greek letter 'D'. The Greeks gave this name to the end of the River Nile because it was triangular shaped, like a capital letter delta (Δ). The word is now used for all river deltas.

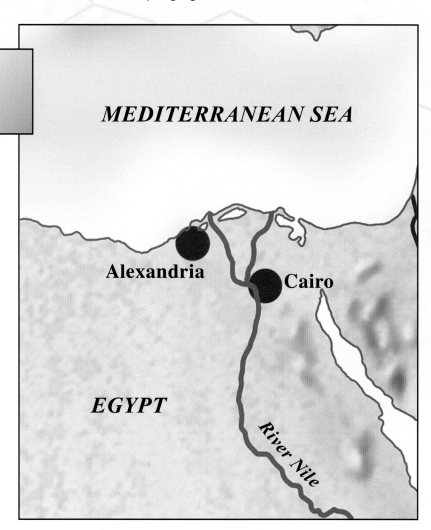

MEDITERRANEAN SEA

Alexandria

Cairo

EGYPT

River Nile

The Nile delta reaches inland to a point just north of Cairo – a distance of around 100 miles (160 kilometres). Along the coast it stretches a distance of about 155 miles (250 kilometres) between Port Said in the east and Alexandria in the west. Alexandria acts as a gateway for the produce of the delta region and to the River Nile in general. The city was founded by, and named after, the Macedonian Greek conqueror Alexander the Great in 332 BC. He conquered Egypt and chose the location of Alexandria for his new capital city. It was linked to the Nile by a canal and had a large natural harbour on the Mediterranean coast. This meant that it was ideal for trade between the Nile valley and delta and the lands of southern Europe.

Alexander never actually lived in his city and died just nine years after founding it. He was returned to Alexandria, where his body was preserved in a glass coffin encased in gold. His tomb has never been found. Alexander was succeeded by another Greek ruler, Ptolemy I. He was the first of many rulers to control Egypt and the River Nile during what is called the Ptolemaic era (323–30 BC). During this period Alexandria grew into a large and wealthy city. The key to its success was its position as the gateway to the Nile, just as Alexander had foreseen. Within just one hundred years of its foundation it was the greatest city of the ancient world.

The lands of the Nile delta are a fertile farming area, supplying much of Egypt's food and many crops for export.

Paper, grain and cotton

Alexandria is famous as an ancient centre of learning. Much of this fame came about because Alexandria had access to a form of early paper, called **papyrus**. Papyrus was made from a reed of the same name that grew alongside the Nile in the delta region. The stem of the reed was split into thin strips that were then pressed together and dried to form a single sheet of papyrus. Many of the world's greatest scholars studied in Alexandria including the mathematician Archimedes, who invented a device for drawing water from the Nile to water farmers' fields, and the geographer Ptolemy, who produced one of the earliest maps of the Nile.

The many documents created in Alexandria were stored in a great library. At its peak the library held some 700,000 papyrus scrolls, but unfortunately most of this was lost in 48 BC when a fire destroyed the library.

This seal shows the grand buildings of Alexandria as they would have been at the height of its power.

332BC	323-30BC	48BC
Alexandria is founded by Alexander the Great.	Alexandria grows into a large and wealthy city.	Fire destroys Alexandria's library.

The modern port of Alexandria is the most important in Egypt, handling 75 per cent of all Egypt's foreign trade.

When the last of the Ptolemaic rulers, Cleopatra, died in 30 BC Egypt became part of the Roman Empire. Alexandria remained the capital of Egypt and continued to grow under the Romans. It became a centre for transporting grain between Egypt and Rome. The Romans needed vast quantities of grain to keep their troops well fed and came to depend heavily on the **granaries** of Alexandria and the Nile. This ensured that Alexandria remained an important city until near the end of the Roman Empire.

In around AD 640 the Romans lost control of Egypt to Islamic forces from Syria. They chose a new capital, Al-Fustat, which was close to modern-day Cairo. They also moved the main port to Rosetta. As a result, Alexandria fell into a decline that was to last until the rule of Muhammad Ali (1805–48). Muhammad Ali wanted to make Egypt into a great **maritime** power and chose Alexandria as the country's main port. Most importantly, however, he built a new canal linking the city to the Nile – the Muhammadiyah Canal. This coincided with the start of cotton **cultivation** in Egypt. Cotton was introduced into Egypt by the British and came from Pakistan and India. The Nile delta region was ideally suited to growing cotton, and cotton was shipped from Alexandria to the cotton mills of England. The city became prosperous and is today the second-largest city in Egypt, with a population of around 6.5 million. It is a modern industrial city, but still relies heavily on its links with the Nile.

30BC	c AD640	1805-1848
Egypt becomes part of the Roman Empire.	Islamic forces from Syria take control of Egypt and Alexandria falls into decline.	The reign of Muhammad Ali, during which time the Muhammadiyah Canal is built.

Cairo: a mega-city

City of the Nile

Cairo is quite literally built around the Nile. Some parts of the city are even built on islands in the middle of the river. The earliest **settlements** in the area were small farming villages. Settlements similar to these can still be seen on the extreme outskirts of the city. The key to Cairo's growth was its particular location on the river. It is located at the meeting point of two **fertile** farming areas – the Nile valley upstream and the Nile **delta** downstream. With the rest of Egypt being mainly desert, the population of the country has always been crowded into the land surrounding the Nile. Cairo's position between these two areas made it an obvious location for controlling both the people and the trade of the River Nile.

Cairo, in Egypt, is the biggest city on the Nile.

The first major settlement in the Cairo region was at Memphis, located around 14 miles (22 kilometres) to the south of the present city centre. It was founded as the Egyptian capital in around 3100 BC and remained the capital city for about 1000 years. It was from Memphis that early **pharaohs** built the pyramids at nearby Giza. Both Giza and Memphis are today part of the Cairo urban area. During the later periods of ancient Egypt, Memphis lost much of its power to new capitals in Thebes (Luxor) and Alexandria. However, its position on the Nile always ensured it remained an important **administrative** and military centre.

MEDITERRANEAN SEA

Alexandria

Giza

Cairo

Memphis

EGYPT

River Nile

Luxor

This satellite image shows the Nile delta in the bottom centre and the Nile valley on the right. Cairo rests where these two areas join.

An Islamic city

The city of Cairo itself was founded in AD 969 by Islamic rulers known as the Fatamids. Egypt first came under Muslim control in AD 639, when Arabic conquerors defeated the Romans. To control the Nile region they built a new settlement, which they called 'Al-Fustat', meaning 'the **entrenched** camp'. Under Muslim control Al-Fustat quickly grew into a thriving commercial city. Within just a few generations it had a population of several hundred-thousand people. In AD 969 the Fatamids became the latest of several Islamic rulers to control Egypt. They built a new city outside of Al-Fustat and named it Al-Qahirah, which means 'the victorious'. Al-Qahirah is considered to be the start of Cairo proper and parts of this original city can still be seen today.

FACT

The name Cairo originates from Al-Qahirah. European traders mis-pronounced Al-Qahirah and it gradually became known as Cairo.

The largest settlement

Cairo is by far the largest settlement on the River Nile. It stretches along the Nile for a distance of 20 miles (35 kilometres) and extends to the east and west of the river for several miles. In total, Greater Cairo (the city centre and its suburbs) covers an area of around 136 square miles (353 square kilometres). In 2003 the population of Greater Cairo was known to be at least 10 million people. This makes it one of the world's few mega-cities (cities with over 10 million people). Cairo is still a rapidly growing city, and some estimates suggest that the true population of Greater Cairo may already be nearer 16 million or even higher. Between 2000 and 2015 the city's population is expected to grow by at least 2 million people.

Cairo is dependent on the River Nile in many ways. Around two-thirds of the population rely on water supplies from the Nile for their drinking water. The water is taken to special treatment facilities to be cleaned and made safe for drinking. It is then piped into people's homes or to shared public taps in residential buildings (flats) or on the streets. Water from the Nile is also used by Cairo's

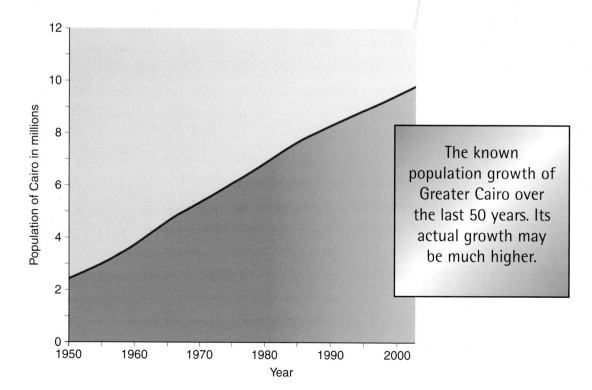

The known population growth of Greater Cairo over the last 50 years. Its actual growth may be much higher.

An industrial district near Cairo. The Nile provides water, electricity and transport for industry.

many industries, such as textiles and the processing of food from the surrounding rural areas. In addition, heavy industries such as engineering, steel and chemical production are found in Cairo. Many of these industries have chosen riverside locations to the north and south of the city centre, to take advantage of the Nile water in their manufacturing processes. The river also provides them with a transportation route for raw materials and finished goods.

As well as taking water from the Nile, Cairo also returns large quantities of used water back into the river. The water is often polluted with waste from homes, factories and industries. This damages the river environment,

killing fish and other river wildlife. They can also pollute the water supplies for people living further downstream. Since 1980 the Egyptian government has been working to reduce the pollution of the Nile. They have passed new laws to ban the dumping of industrial wastes in the river. Although this has improved the situation, large quantities of waste still end up in the Nile. In future, as Cairo's population continues to grow, this problem is set to get even worse.

Bridging the Nile

Before 1964 the western bank of the Nile was frequently flooded by the annual rise of the Nile's waters. Because of this, most of Cairo was built on the eastern side of the river, where the land was a little higher. After 1964 the problem of flooding was controlled by the construction of the Aswan High Dam (see pages 14–15). This opened up the western bank for development and a building boom soon followed. Thousands of new homes were built and small farming villages were quickly swallowed up by the expansion of the city. The western side of Cairo is still growing today. It stretches almost 12 miles (20 kilometres) inland from the Nile to the ancient pyramids of Giza.

A crowded river taxi crosses the Nile in Cairo. Cairo struggles to keep pace with its fast-growing population.

c3100BC	**AD639**	**969**
Memphis is founded as the Egyptian capital.	Egypt comes under Muslim control.	Cairo is founded by the Fatamids.

The Pyramids of Giza

Although surrounded by desert, the pyramids at Giza owe much to the annual flooding of the Nile. The floods covered much of modern-day Giza and brought the Nile almost to the foot of the pyramids. This allowed enormous blocks of stone to be transported to the pyramids by boat, including the limestone from across the Nile at Tura and stone from quarries as far away as Aswan – over 500 miles (800 kilometres) away. Scientists believe that it took at least 20 years and over 20,000 labourers to build each pyramid.

As the population of western Cairo increased there was a need to better connect east and west Cairo across the Nile. This led to the construction of several new bridges. The most important of these is the '6 October Bridge', which was started in 1969. The bridge is unusual in that once it has crossed the Nile, it continues into the heart of eastern Cairo as an elevated highway and handles around half of Cairo's traffic every day – an estimated 40,000 cars per hour. A number of ferries also operate on the Nile carrying passengers across, up and down the river. In a city so divided by its river, these forms of transport are vital to the continuing growth of the Nile's greatest city.

1964	1969	1980
Construction of the Aswan High Dam is started.	'6 October Bridge' started.	Egyptian government begins to reduce the pollution of the Nile.

Khartoum: the meeting of rivers

The elephant's trunk

Khartoum is today the capital city of Sudan, but was once part of an area under Egyptian, and later British, control. It shares its location on the Nile with two other **settlements** – Omdurman and North Khartoum. Together they make up the largest urban centre in Sudan, with a population of around 3.5 million. Although all three settlements have their own characteristics, they are often simply referred to as Khartoum. Khartoum is located at the point where the White Nile and Blue Nile meet and flow as a single river for the first time. Khartoum even takes its name from the piece of land between the rivers where they join. This land is shaped like an elephant's trunk, and it is this that gives the city its Arabic name of 'Al-Khurt um' meaning 'elephant's trunk'. This was later adapted to become Khartoum.

The meeting of the rivers makes Khartoum a key location for controlling movement up and down the rivers. Because of this, in 1821 the Egyptian army established a camp there. The camp quickly developed into a formal settlement and, by the early 1860s, had a population of around 30,000.

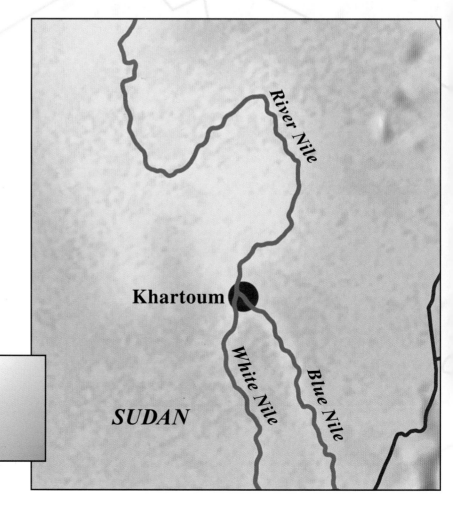

Khartoum is located in central Sudan.

Khartoum also provided a good starting point for exploration into the heart of Africa. Because of this, it became an important trading post – with the trade in slaves and ivory being especially important. Khartoum was also the starting point for Samuel Baker's expedition to find the **source** of the White Nile in 1863.

Slaving on the Nile

Khartoum was a major centre for the African slave trade during the mid-19th century. Slave traders ('slavers') would leave Khartoum with up to 300 armed men, and sail upstream along the White Nile. The slavers would land and raid nearby villages to capture people as slaves, and then ship them back to Khartoum. The slavers would also steal or buy ivory from local chiefs. In a good raid a slaver might return to Khartoum with up to 500 slaves and up to 9000 kilograms of ivory. The ivory and slaves were sold to traders, who then journeyed onwards across the desert to the Red Sea, or down the Nile to Cairo. Slavery on the Nile reached its peak in the 1860s. At this time an estimated 15,000 Arabic slavers were capturing 50,000 slaves a year from the lands of the upper Nile.

Battles on the Nile

In the last decades of the 19th century, Khartoum and Omdurman became the scene of a power struggle between the British authorities and an Islamic religious leader known as the Mahdi. The British had taken control of Khartoum following their invasion of Egypt. The Mahdi rose to power from a small island in the Nile, about 150 miles (240 kilometres) south of Khartoum, gathered support throughout Sudan and soon had a large army under his control. In March 1884 the Mahdi's supporters approached Khartoum and held it under **siege**. The British Governor-General, General Gordon, evacuated around 2000 people before the attack, but refused to surrender to the Mahdi. The long siege began with Gordon trapped in his palace, waiting for support to reach him by the Nile.

In January 1885, after a 10-month siege, 50,000 Mahdi supporters launched a final attack on Khartoum. General Gordon was killed in the attack, along with most of the population of Khartoum.

The tomb of the Mahdi in Omdurman stands as a reminder of the power struggles that took place for the control of Khartoum.

British reinforcements arrived by steamer up the Nile three days too late – Khartoum had already fallen. The British came under fierce attack from the Mahdi's forces and retreated back down the Nile. The Mahdi built a new capital across the river from Khartoum in Omdurman but died just a few months after his victory. His tomb in Omdurman is today a site of pilgrimage for Muslims and a major attraction for visitors to the city.

The Mahdi was succeeded by one of his followers, Khalifa Abdullah. The Khalifa ruled from Omdurman for the next decade and continued to spread the beliefs of the Mahdi. In 1898 his rule was brought to an end by a British force that travelled up the Nile by steamboat. General Horatio Kitchener and his forces reached Omdurman on 1 September and quickly overpowered the Khalifa's forces.

As stability returned to the region, Khartoum was again declared the capital of the area and soon began to grow as the traders returned. Kitchener was given the job of rebuilding Khartoum. He laid out a city of wide tree-lined avenues that survive to this day. Many fine buildings were constructed during this period and a new industrial area began to develop in what became North Khartoum.

By 1902 Khartoum had also become a centre of learning, with its own college that later became the University of Khartoum. Trade continued to be the main activity in Khartoum, and the Nile was used to transport goods. Textiles, leather-goods, and **gum Arabic** were among the region's most important commodities.

The Gezira project

Today, Khartoum is still dominated by the Nile, because its economy remains heavily dependent on agriculture. The most important agricultural region is called Gezira. It is a large area of land south of Khartoum, sandwiched between the White Nile and the Blue Nile. The Gezira project was started by the British in 1911, to grow cotton for England's textile mills. In 1925 the Sennar Dam was built across the Blue Nile. This diverted river water into a system of **irrigation** canals and to the fields of Gezira. The extra water led to a massive expansion in the scheme, which the Sudanese government continued when the country became independent in 1956.

A worker allows Nile waters onto the irrigated fields of the Gezira project.

By the 1970s the Gezira scheme covered an area of 2.5 million acres and provided water for over 100,000 **tenant farmers**. As the area of the scheme increased, so too did the network of canals and ditches that transported water from the Blue Nile to the fields. Today, this network stretches for around 2700 miles (4350 kilometres).

1821	1885	1898	1902
Egyptian army establishes a camp at Khartoum.	Mahdi forces defeat the British at Khartoum. The capital is moved from Khartoum to Omdurman.	British forces overpower Khalifa's at Omdurman. Khartoum becomes the capital again.	Khartoum has its own college.

Refugees from countries suffering drought have fled to Khartoum, so the city continues to expand.

This makes it one of the biggest irrigation schemes in the world. Cotton remains the most important crop grown on the Gezira project. The raw cotton is taken to Khartoum for processing and is then exported to markets around the world. Other crops grown at Gezira include peanuts, millet, sorghum, wheat and different types of vegetables. Most of these are taken to markets in Khartoum for feeding the growing local population. The Gezira project is one of the best examples of how the Nile can bring great benefits. Without it, there would be less food available and the many industrial jobs that depend on Gezira would not exist.

City of refugees

During the 1970s and 1980s, Sudan and its neighbouring countries suffered a series of droughts and conflicts. These severely disrupted food supplies in the region and led to terrible famines. Millions of people were forced from their homes to search for food and water, and hundreds of thousands died. Many of the refugees headed for Khartoum and the city's population grew rapidly. At the start of the 1970s Khartoum's population was 665,000, but by the end of the 1980s it had increased to over 1.8 million. The River Nile was an important attraction for people, because even in the very worst of droughts the Nile continues to flow. Many of the refugees settled in Khartoum and have never returned to their homes.

1911	1925	1970–1980s
Gezira project started by the British.	Sennar Dam built across the Blue Nile.	Refugees flood into Khartoum because of droughts in Sudan and neighbouring countries.

Jinja: source of the Nile

'A stone'

Jinja is located in Uganda at the point where the White Nile leaves Lake Victoria. The town is highly dependent on the river and lake. They provide people with transport, energy, food and jobs. Even the name 'Jinja' is related to the river. It come comes from the word 'ejjinja' in the local Luganda language, which translates to 'a stone'. It is said to refer to a single stone that stands close to Ripon Falls – the waterfalls that John Hanning Speke believed were the **source** of the Nile (see page 5). A plaque marks the spot where Speke is said to have made his discovery on 28 July 1862. Although later evidence shows that Ripon Falls are not the ultimate source of the White Nile, they are still important as the visible start of the White Nile.

The area that is now Jinja was little more than a few fishing and farming **settlements** until the beginning of the 20th century. At this time the British controlled Uganda as part of their **colonial empire** in Africa and in 1901 established Jinja as an **administration** and trading post. Jinja soon became of great importance to the British as a

Jinja is in Uganda on the edge of Lake Victoria.

FACT

It takes around three months for the water entering the Nile at Jinja to reach the Mediterranean Sea.

UGANDA

White Nile

Jinja

Kampala

Kisumu

Lake Victoria

RWANDA

BURUNDI

TANZANIA

port for transporting Ugandan goods back to England. The goods were taken by steamboats from Jinja across Lake Victoria to Kisumu, in neighbouring Kenya. In Kisumu they were transferred to rail for the journey to the ocean port of Mombasa. Among the most important goods transported in this way were cotton and coffee.

THIS SPOT
MARKS THE PLACE FROM WHERE
THE NILE STARTS ITS LONG JOURNEY
TO THE MEDITERRANEAN SEA THROUGH
CENTRAL AND NORTHERN UGANDA
SUDAN AND EGYPT

A plaque marking the spot where the source of the Nile was believed to be.

The East Africa Railway

*The East Africa Railway was started in 1896 as part of an ambitious British plan to link Mombasa on the Kenyan coast to the **fertile** lands of Lake Victoria and the Nile. By 1901 the railway reached Lake Victoria at Kisumu. In 1910 the railway was extended from Jinja to Namisagali, a settlement further along the River Nile, where it enters Lake Kyoga. This new rail line allowed cotton grown along the Nile and around Lake Kyoga to be transported to the port in Jinja. Trade between the Nile region and Mombasa increased and a new section of railway was built to connect Jinja directly to Mombasa in 1928. The East Africa Railway is still in use today, although much of it has fallen into disrepair as road transport has become more popular.*

The power of water

Jinja grew rapidly after the construction of the Owen Falls Dam, which was completed in 1954. The dam was built a little over a mile (about 2 kilometres) downstream of where the Nile leaves Lake Victoria. As the waters behind the dam rose, Ripon Falls were flooded and are no longer visible. The main purpose of the Owen Falls Dam was to generate electricity for Uganda. As the water passes through the dam it turns giant **turbines** that generate power. This is then transferred by power lines across the country.

Cheap electricity from the Owen Falls Dam and a plentiful supply of water made Jinja a good place to set up factories. Jinja soon became the most important industrial town in Uganda. Textile factories, iron **foundries**, **tanneries**, a sugar **refinery** and a brewery are among the industries that have been set up in Jinja since the building of the Owen Falls Dam. All of these need large quantities of water and electricity as part of their production process. Of course the dam itself is also an important industry, providing electricity to Uganda and neighbouring Kenya.

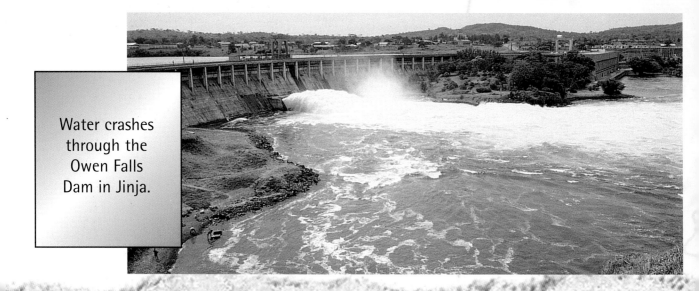

Water crashes through the Owen Falls Dam in Jinja.

1862	1896	1901
John Hanning Speke discovers the source of the Nile.	East Africa Railway started.	The British establish Jinja as an administration and trading post.

The Bujagali Falls in Jinja are sometimes used for white-water rafting, and are threatened by plans for a reservoir.

Jobs provided by the new industries in Jinja have led to a growth in the population of the town. By 2002 there were just over 100,000 people living in the town. Many thousands more live in the surrounding villages and travel into Jinja to work each day.

In 2001 a second dam was built alongside the original Owen Falls Dam. This helped to increase the amount of power produced, but Uganda still suffers from a shortage of electricity. Because of this there are now plans to build another dam across the Nile, around 4 miles (7 kilometres) downstream of the Owen Falls Dam. The plans for the new dam are very unpopular with people living alongside the river. Many of them are likely to see their homes and their land disappear under the reservoir created by the new dam.

The Nile at this point also attracts thousands of tourists each year. Most come to see the spectacular force of the Nile as it cascades through a series of spectacular rapids. They can also test their wits against the river by going white-water rafting down the rapids. If the new dam is built then these rapids will be lost beneath the new reservoir. This could destroy the tourism industry in Jinja, which employs hundreds of people and is heavily focused on the Nile.

1928	1954	2001
New section of railway links Jinja and Mombasa.	Completion of the Owen Falls Dam at Jinja.	Second dam built at Owen Falls.

The Nile of tomorrow

The Nile is a truly remarkable river. For much of its length it flows through a land that is desert to either side. And yet it supports millions of people on some of the most **fertile** farmland in the world and in one of its biggest cities – Cairo. Nowhere is the dependence on the Nile more obvious than in Egypt. The ancient Egyptians linked their gods to the Nile, thanking it for their very existence. Their entire lives were based around the Nile floods and the good fortune it brought to their land. Though the force of the Nile is now controlled by the Aswan High Dam it continues to dominate Egyptian life. It provides Egyptians with water, with power and with transportation. Without the Nile, Egypt as we know it today would simply not exist. It is little wonder then that Egypt is often referred to as 'the gift of the Nile'.

People have been drawn to settle on the banks of the Nile since ancient times. Today, villages line its banks from **source** to **mouth**,

The Nile at Aswan still attracts people today as it has done for thousands of years.

but it is the big **settlements** that now dominate life on the Nile. The earliest of these were founded to control trade along the Nile. At the time of their foundation the Nile provided the only known route into the heart of Africa. The riches of gold, ivory and spices that could be found there made control of the Nile one of the great prizes in the world. Civilizations and empires struggled for control of the Nile right up until the middle of the 20th century. Their different influences are clearly visible in the buildings and layouts of the Nile's settlements today.

But what does the future hold for the settlements of the Nile? As populations continue to grow, one of the main challenges will be to satisfy the many different demands on the Nile's life-giving waters. People will need more water for their homes, for growing crops, for their industries and for generating power. They will also produce more waste which, if not carefully handled, could find its way back into the Nile and pollute its waters.

Uganda, Ethiopia and Egypt all have plans to use the waters of the Nile in ways that could reduce the amount of water reaching settlements downstream. Some scientists have suggested that with so much water

Village life along the Nile continues in much the same way as it has for hundreds of years.

being taken from the Nile it may soon dry up before it reaches the sea. Just as the Nile has brought life to the people living alongside it, the river is now reliant on people to keep it healthy for the future. The relationship may be changing, but the link between the Nile and its people is as strong as it has ever been.

Timeline

c 3100 BC	Memphis is founded as the Egyptian capital.
2613–2494	Pyramids at Giza are built.
2040–1069	Thebes (Luxor) becomes an increasingly important city.
2000	Earlier parts of the temple of Karnak are built.
1475	**Obelisks** transported to Luxor for the temple of Karnak.
332	Alexandria is founded by Alexander the Great.
323–30	Alexandria grows into a large and wealthy city.
30	Egypt becomes part of the Roman Empire.
c AD639	Egypt under Muslim control. Alexandria in decline.
969	Cairo is founded by the Fatamids.
1805–1848	The Muhammadiyah Canal is built at Alexandria.
1821	Egyptian army establishes a camp at Khartoum.
1860s	Slavery on the Nile reaches its peak.
1862	John Hanning Speke discovers the **source** of the Nile.
1863	Samuel Baker's expedition to find the source of the White Nile.
1885	Sudan's capital is moved from Khartoum to Omdurman.
1896	East Africa Railway started.
1898	British forces move Sudan's capital back to Khartoum.
1901	Jinja is established as an **administration** and trading post.
1902	First dam at Aswan completed by the British.
1911	Gezira project started by the British.
1922	Howard Carter discovers the tomb of Tutankhamun.
1925	Sennar Dam built across the Blue Nile.
1928	New section of railway links Jinja and Mombasa.
1954	Construction of the Owen Falls Dam at Jinja.
1964	Construction of the Aswan High Dam is started.
1969	'6 October Bridge' started.
1970–1980s	Refugees from Sudan flood into Khartoum.
1971	Aswan High Dam completed.
1980	Egyptian government starts reducing Nile pollution.

Further resources

Books

A River Journey: The Nile,
Rob Bowden (Hodder Wayland 2003)

Great Cities of the World: Cairo,
Rob Bowden and Roy Maconachie
(World Almanac Library, 2004)

Green Alert: Polluted Waters,
Jennifer Stefanow (Raintree, 2004)

Take Your Camera to Egypt,
Ted Park (Raintree, 2003)

Websites

Thebes
(**www.thebanmappingproject.com/**)
Superb website with information on Thebes
and valley of kings – interactive videos and maps
make it highly accessible and very informative.

Egypt
(**magma.nationalgeographic.com/ngm/egypt/**)
National Geographic website celebrating the
treasures of Egypt – guides to the pyramids and
a map of the Nile as it passes through Egypt.

Nile Basin
(**www.nilebasin.org/IntroNR.htm**)
This web page provides a useful snapshot overview
of the River Nile and includes a link to a very good
map of the river and its major settlements.

River Nile
(**www.sis.gov.eg/egyptinf/culture/html/rnile.htm**)
This page is provided by the Egyptian government
and provides an overview of the importance of the
River Nile to the country and people of Egypt.

Glossary

administration/administrative concerning management and control. An administration centre is somewhere that decisions are made and records are kept.

archaeologist scientist who finds and examines evidence from the past that is often buried in the ground

colonial empire group of nations, areas or peoples (the colonized) ruled by one major power (the colonizer). Britain had a major colonial empire until the early 1900s and controlled large parts of the world including Egypt, Uganda and Sudan.

cultivation preparing and using the soil for growing crops

delta area at the mouth of a river, formed by sand and soil being deposited in a triangular shape

drought period in which rainfall falls below that normally expected. A long period of drought can severely affect farming and lead to food shortages and famine.

entrenched establishing something so firmly it is difficult for it to be changed

erode the wearing away of rock and soil by wind, water, ice or acid

famine shortage of food that leads to hunger and in severe cases may result in death. Famine is often caused by drought or by conflicts, which disrupt food supplies.

fertile rich soil in which crops can grow easily

foundry building (factory) in which metal is cast (made)

granary a storehouse for threshing grain (separating off grain)

gum Arabic water-based gum from acacia trees used as a glue and to thicken food

irrigation watering crops using specially created systems. Normally used in areas of low rainfall.

maritime to do with the sea

mortuary building where dead bodies are kept and prepared for burial or cremation

mouth ending point of a river

necropolis ancient cemetery

nutrients substance that feeds and provides the energy needed for growth

obelisk square-sided pillar carved into a pyramid shape at the top

papyrus a reed that grows in waterlogged land along the River Nile. Stems of the fully grown plants are used to make boats and the insides are used to make a form of early paper.

pharaoh king of ancient Egypt

Re Sun god and father of the gods. In ancient Egypt, Re was the creator of all life on earth and in heaven.

reaches sections of a river (upper, middle and lower reaches)

refinery a factory where a raw material, such as crude oil, is changed into other useful materials, such as petrol

refugees people forced to flee their natural home because of war or natural threats such as drought, flooding or earthquakes, in order to protect their lives

sediment fine particles of soil and rock that are eroded (worn away) by the force of water and carried in a river or stream before being deposited further downstream

Semitic family of languages from North Africa and south-western Asia. They include the Hebrew, Arabic, Aramaic and Maltese languages.

settlement place that has people living in it permanently. Settlements can vary in size from a small village to a large city.

siege surrounding of a city or castle by an army wanting to capture it

source starting point of a river

tannery a place where animal skin is converted into leather

tenant farmers farmers who rent the land being farmed

turbine a motor that is turned by steam or water

water table level in the ground. Below it the rocks and soil are filled with water.

wharf a level area along a river or sea to which a ship may moor to load and unload

Index